CLASS 43 LOCOMOTIVES IN SCOTLAND

THE HIGH SPEED TRAINS

COLIN J. HOWAT

AMBERLEY

First published 2025

Amberley Publishing
The Hill, Stroud
Gloucestershire, GL5 4EP

www.amberley-books.com

ISBN 978 1 3981 2459 2 (print)
ISBN 978 1 3981 2460 8 (ebook)

British Library Cataloguing in Publication Data.
A catalogue record for this book is available from the British Library.

Typesetting by Hurix Digital, India.
Printed in the UK.

Appointed GPSR EU Representative: Easy Access System Europe Oü, 16879218
Address: Mustamäe tee 50, 10621, Tallinn, Estonia
Contact Details: gpsr.requests@easproject.com, +358 40 500 3575

Introduction

After the Second World War the desire for more rail travel within the United Kingdom increased. The railway modernisation plan of the mid-1950s which eventually led to the withdrawal of steam power identified the need for more modern diesel and electric traction. The development of the motorway system had started and began to have an effect on the British Rail (BR) network. The 1960s West Coast Main Line modernisation plans with electrification had brought journey times down between London and northern cities such as Liverpool and Manchester. Other indications of changes came in the shape of the introduction of a fully air-conditioned new train built by Metro-Cammell called the 'Blue Pullman', which were introduced between London St Pancras and Manchester Central. These high-quality trains with their streamlined power cars and excellent rolling stock were a forerunner to the later developments of the Class 43 High Speed Train (HST). In the UK some benefits came to long-distance trains from the Inter City branding, but due to a lack of government investment for the railway, almost no real investment was made in the UK railways from the 1960s onwards. The anti-rail governments of the period put a stop to any plans to develop a UK version of the Japanese High Speed Train Networks, even though the cost per mile on a new twin-track railway was less than half that of a motorway.

In 1967 the first steps towards developing a HST began to take shape. The appointment of Walter Jowett as Director of Design within British Rail was made. He came from a railway engineering background having worked with the English Electric Company. He was tasked with taking BR into the 1970s with modern diesel traction developments. In August 1969 the HST concept was further defined and called for power cars on a fixed train formation to be provided at either end. The British Railways Board (BRB) stated that the HST was meant to be a stopgap until the Advanced Passenger Trains (APT) were ready. The Derby-based Research and Development Centre were entrusted with the structural design of the HST. The power cars would be of a new design mounted on a Bo-Bo wheel configuration. The front end would be streamlined whilst the inner end would have a slab coach end fitted with a connecting gangway to the passenger coaches. Two power cars were deemed necessary at the time due to the power required as there were no diesel engines capable of producing more than 4,500 horsepower. It also meant more flexibility at stations as it removed the need for another loco to be attached for the next working. Assembly of the first two prototype power cars was undertaken at BR Engineering Works at Crewe and they were numbered 41001 and 41002. The cab design was new to the UK and was met initially with resistance by the train drivers' union ASLEF. Provision was made for a driver's assistant seat in the early days of operation. However, ASLEF insisted that any HSTs that travelled over 100 mph were required to be double manned for safety reasons. This was eventually accepted by BR management as the unions were threatening to boycott the sets. Dynamic testing started on the East Coast Main Line from January 1973. Some faults were identified including problems with the power units and turbochargers. Bogie hunting was also experienced and a severe burning smell from the brake pads occurred especially when heavy braking was done. During the early days of trials on the East Coast Main Line (ECML), the prototype HST was outbased at Leeds' Neville Hill Depot. On 10 June 1973 a test HST obtained the then diesel world record for speed when it reached 141 mph (227 kmph) between Thirsk and Tollerton.

On 2 August 1973 a press run was also organised with railway staff between London Kings Cross and Darlington. This included the then BRB Chairman Sir Richard Marsh and various other well-known MPs. The trip operated well and received good reviews from the press. By early 1974 the first production HSTs were under construction for the Western Region. The prototype was then transferred to Old Oak Common Depot in London. The original Class 41 designation was upgraded and any new power cars coming off the production line were renumbered in the 43xxx series. The first production set entered service on the Western Region on 4 December 1974. In August 1975, the prototype set now numbered 252001 was sent to Shildon to take part in the celebrations to mark the 150th anniversary of the railways. The cavalcade had started off with a replica of Stephenson's *Rocket* steam loco right through the different time periods up to and including the HST. With the success of the Great Western sets, the BRB requested more for the Eastern and Scottish routes including CrossCountry workings. The initial request was for 161 sets in total but the government eventually only gave the go ahead for ninety-five. While the prototype set was under construction, engineers at the Derby RTC upgraded the design for the production batches. Much was learnt from the test runs and a number of changes were incorporated into the production fleet. It was agreed with ASLEF that the driving cabs would now be equipped with two seats and new cab side windows. Exterior design of the power cars was refined and upgraded by industrial designer Kenneth Grange, who came up with a couple of bright ideas. He streamlined the appearance of the power cars with a two-tone livery whilst generating the appearance of speed, efficiency and presence. The buffers were removed, the marker lights were made more streamlined and the nose end connections were hidden under a hinged panel. This meant that an attachable bar for assistance could also be hidden and only brought out when a set was required to be assisted clear from the main line. The horns were also repositioned from roof height to just below the front windscreen to reduce internal cab noise. The provision of cab side windows made a major improvement in light distribution. A redesigned bogie classified as BP16 was now used with a more robust structure and improved riding qualities.

The interior of the production power cars followed largely that of the prototype with a slightly altered cab area. The radiators were repositioned towards the power unit and the recessed floor on the prototype was replaced with a flat area. It was also agreed that the production HSTs would be used in semi-permanent formed sets. The guards accommodation area at the inner end of the power car was to be short lived as after intervention by the NUR, a guards area was to be provided in the standard MK3 coaches instead. This would also incorporate an office and luggage area. The inclusion of the full guards compartment had been included in power cars 43002 to 43152. These were classified Driving Motor Brakes (DMBs). Nos 43153–43198 were fitted with luggage space only and no guards equipment and were thus classified as a Driving Motor Cars (DMCs) only. The equipment was progressively removed from 43002 to 43152 after 1986. As with the prototypes, the production power cars were built at Crewe Works and the passenger stock at Derby Litchurch Lane Works. The HST trailer coaches were basically loco-hauled MK3s with on-board power systems supplied by a three-phase train line usually fed by one power car. Each coach had an air-conditioning unit powered by the three-phase train lighting circuitry. Coaches were mounted on BT10 bogies with secondary suspension provided by air springs. Each axle had individual disc brakes and a linkage from the levelling device of the air suspension that controlled the brake pressure via a load proportional valve.

At an early stage in construction, it was announced that the production trains would be classified 253 for the Western Region and 254 for the Eastern and Scottish Regions. Passengers did not have to wait long to be able to sample high-speed running at 125 mph (201 kmph) when services on the Western Region commenced in October 1976. Twenty-seven sets were then allocated to the Eastern Region while five sets, Nos 254016–020 (43086–43095), were allocated to Craigentinny Depot in Scotland. The first HSTs were due to be launched in May 1978 on the London Kings Cross to Newcastle workings, followed by Edinburgh and later to Aberdeen and Inverness. Thirty-two sets were made available by early 1979 and a high-profile launch for the new ECML service was planned from May 1979. However, this had to be abandoned following the collapse of the Penmanshiel Tunnel, south of Dunbar, when a section of the roof collapsed killing two engineers during a possession. The tunnel had been getting upgraded to allow the passage of container trains. This major collapse severed the East Coast Main Line, which required a new route to be built around the tunnel area. It also required the nearby A1 road to be realigned. During this period of closure, certain services, mainly freights and sleepers, were diverted via the West Coast Main Line and on several occasions via the G&SW to get to/from Edinburgh. After their introduction from May 1979, the performance of the HSTs was good and the 10.00 Kings Cross to Edinburgh became the 'Flying Scotsman', the fastest of all the HST services to London, taking just four hours and thirty-seven minutes for the trip with just one intermediate stop at Newcastle. Due to this success, the BRB submitted further plans for HSTs to be introduced between London Paddington and Penzance and authorisation was given by the government for an additional fourteen sets to be built. The fourth area to be requested by the BRB for HSTs was the CrossCountry sector linking Aberdeen all the way via various cities as far west as Penzance. This operation was later managed from Birmingham and other routes such as Bournemouth and Poole joined the HST network. Thirty-six additional sets were ordered. The first batch would cover the Edinburgh/Newcastle to Leeds, on to Derby and Birmingham, then onwards to Cardiff, Plymouth and Penzance. The second batch would cover routes from Glasgow Central, Liverpool and Manchester to Birmingham and various points west towards Poole, Bournemouth, Portsmouth and Brighton. Most of these services started up from May 1982. In 1981 Cyril Bleasdale was appointed as Business Director for InterCity and he announced that the Midland Main Line would also benefit from HST sets. After a lot of reshuffling of the sets, most of these services were taken over by HSTs from the end of 1982. In 1983 following pressure from various Scottish Highland councils, a HST service to Inverness was provided. From May 1984, a new revamped 'Highland Chieftain' service was launched between Inverness and London Kings Cross. After privatisation of the UK network from June 1994, the HST fleet became the property of two leasing companies, Porterbrook and Angel. In Scotland this meant services continued to operate from Edinburgh, Aberdeen and Inverness by GNER via the ECML, whilst other services between Aberdeen, Dundee, Edinburgh and Glasgow Central were operated by InterCity CrossCountry.

On the ECML, HSTs were beginning to be replaced themselves in 1989 by Class 91s with DVTs. Eventually by 2019, Hitachi 801 series trains then began to replace the Class 91s and the final timetabled HST service with GNER ran on 15 December 2019 when it worked the 19.35 Kings Cross to Leeds service. Virgin Trains were granted the CrossCountry and West Coast franchises from May 1996. However, as part of their franchise bid, they were committed to introduce new rolling stock and phase out the HSTs. This was undertaken with fleets of Voyager Class 220 and 221 stock for CrossCountry workings and Class 390s for the WCML. This meant that the HSTs of Virgin and other operators began to be stored at numerous locations around the UK. As time progressed new operators were found for them. This included Grand Central, Network Rail and others. On 11 November 2007, under a franchise change, the CrossCountry operation was taken over by Arriva Trains. They continued to operate HSTs with a number of sets being based at Edinburgh Craigentinny Depot. After the transfer of this depot to Hitachi in 2015 and as a part of the East Coast modernisation, the CrossCountry HST fleet were further transferred to Plymouth Laira Depot. Soon after this the MK3 coaches were upgraded at Wabtec Doncaster when sliding passenger doors and retention toilet tanks were fitted, a project that was completed by the spring of 2020. Open Access operator Grand Central entered the HST business in 2006 after being given paths for services between Sunderland and London Kings Cross. However, there was insufficient HST coaching stock initially available and a number of MK3 loco-hauled coaches were purchased and upgraded to HST standards by Axiom Rail based at Stoke.

With surplus HST power cars and coaches, Network Rail took advantage of the position and leased a number of vehicles to form a new Network Measurement Train (NMT) – a self-contained HST set able to monitor and detect track irregularities at line speed. MK2 and MK3 coaches were modified by Hunslet Barclay at Kilmarnock and at the Railway Technical Centre in Derby. In 2019 the new ScotRail franchise was awarded to Abellio, who sought new trains for its domestic InterCity services. It was decided to transfer fifty-four power cars from the Great Western region with associated MK3 coaching stock. These new ScotRail sets were to be in 2+4 and 2+5 formations and were known as the Inter7City sets. A major refurbishment contract undertaken by Wabtec was arranged. Coaches were refurbished at Kilmarnock and Doncaster and the power cars were upgraded at Brush Loughborough. Crewe based Locomotive Services Ltd (LSL) also purchased a number of out of service HST power cars and coaches in 2020 and subsequently formed up the 2+9 Midland Pullman set. It was delivered to Crewe in October 2020 and has worked over many routes in Scotland since. Due to the increase in coaching stock and power cars in the ScotRail franchise, Cadder Yard on the north side of Glasgow was upgraded to a HST depot and opened in 2021 to cope with the demand, with all main repairs being carried out at Haymarket Depot. Eastfield Depot, north of Queen Street, had already been expanded to cope with Class 170 Turbostars and later Electric Class 385s but had simply run out of space for the HST sets.

Depot Codes

BG – Bounds Green (BR)
EC – Edinburgh Craigentinny (BR/GNER/LNER)
DT – Derby Research Centre
DR – Direct Rail Services Carlisle
EC – Edinburgh Craigentinny (BR/GNER/LNER)
HA – Haymarket (ScotRail)
IS – Inverness
LS – Locomotive Services Crewe
NL – Leeds Neville Hill

2+8 set crosses the Montrose Basin Girder Bridge on the single line between Montrose and Usan with an Aberdeen to Kings Cross service. (October 1979)

2+8 set at Carstairs, set No. 254017 (EC). This set had been on a shuttle service from Edinburgh. This was due to the ECML being closed, a reaction to the Penmanshiel Tunnel having collapsed. Passengers off this connected into a Central to Birmingham New Street service. (July 1979)

HST and a Class 40 share duties at Aberdeen. The Class 40 had just brought in a service from Queen Street and the HST was about to depart with a service to Edinburgh with No. 254019 (EC). (August 1980)

2+8 set arrives at Arbroath with an Aberdeen to Kings Cross service, set No. 254018 (EC). Note the old station barrow on the right. (August 1980)

2+8 set passes the old Aberdeen South signal box near the station with a service to Kings Cross. The semaphores were replaced by coloured lights in September of the same year. (August 1980)

2+8 set crosses the South Esk Viaduct on the single line between Montrose and Usan with an Aberdeen to Kings Cross service. (October 1979)

2+8 set arrives at Edinburgh with a Leeds to Aberdeen service formed by set No. 254031 (NH). Note the parcel vans in the north sidings. These sidings were removed in 2003 and replaced with a new platform. (June 1980)

2+8 set at Queen Street. This set had arrived on a service from Edinburgh and would then depart for Kings Cross. There appeared to be a problem with the front of power car No. 43088 (EC). (July 1981)

2+8 set passes Slochd Summit near Aviemore with a Kings Cross to Inverness service, power car No. 43108 (NL) leading. (June 1992/Roddy MacPhee)

2+8 set passes Polmadie Depot on the south side of Glasgow with a diverted Central to Kings Cross service. Queen Street had been closed due to engineering work. Note the Class 83 and 87 coupled up to ECS in the Down sidings. (April 1982)

2+8 set passes Kinnaber Junction north of Montrose with an Aberdeen to Kings Cross service. Note the lines on the left. At one time these ran through to Perth. However, by this time they only served local customers at Brechin and the line was closed completely shortly after this shot was taken. (November 1980)

2+8 set at Edinburgh with a service to Kings Cross. Note the BRUTES on the left with the south platform lines to the right. Note also that part of the horn grille protector in the trailing power car was missing. (February 1986)

2+8 set at Lairgo between Stonehaven and Montrose with an Aberdeen to Kings Cross service, set number 254035 (EC) at the time. Note the Grampian Hills in the background. (December 1982)

2+4 set arrives at Stirling with an Aberdeen to Queen Street service, power car 43183 (HA) leading. (September 2023)

2+8 set arrives at Montrose with the 0840 Aberdeen to Kings Cross service. The bay platforms were used by fertiliser and other traffic at the time but only one siding now survives. (August 1982)

2+4 set at Daviot south of Inverness with a Queen Street to Inverness service, power car 43163 (HA) leading. (August 2019/Roddy MacPhee)

2+8 set crosses the Forth Bridge with the 1600 Aberdeen to Kings Cross service. The bridge was built between 1882 and 1889. (April 1987)

2+8 set in original BR livery emerges out of Princess Street Gardens in Edinburgh with an Aberdeen to Kings Cross service. (May 1986)

2+9 set near Culloden Viaduct south of Inverness with an Inverness to Kings Cross service, power car 43274 (NL) trailing. (July 2018/Roddy MacPhee)

2+8 set near Burnmouth with the 1000 Kings Cross to Edinburgh service 'The Flying Scotsman'. (July 1981)

2+4 set arrives at Inverkeithing with an Aberdeen to Edinburgh service, power car 43141 (HA) leading. (August 2023)

2+9 set at Moy near Aviemore with an Inverness to Kings Cross service, power car 43316 (NL) leading. (March 2013/Roddy MacPhee)

2+8 set passes Laurencekirk signal box with an Aberdeen to Kings Cross service. The disused station was behind the camera. It was re-opened in May 2009. (May 1983)

2+7 set, PC 43084 (NH) trailing passes through Carluke station with a service from Newcastle to Glasgow Central. (April 1991)

2+8 set near Wallyford with an Aberdeen to Kings Cross service, power car 43106 (BG) leading. A new station was re-opened near this location in June 1994. (March 1988/Roddy MacPhee)

2+5 set at Perth with a Queen Street to Aberdeen service, power car 43026 (HA) trailing. (July 2023)

2+8 set north of Arbroath with an Aberdeen to Kings Cross service. Note the two first-class coaches and two buffet cars behind the power car. These formations were altered to one each and replaced by standard coaches to improve capacity after a few years due to poor patronage. (May 1982)

2+8 set passes the site of the Penmanshiel Tunnel near Grantshouse with the 1245 Edinburgh to Kings Cross service. The ECML had to be re-alinged after the tunnel collapsed in March 1979. (July 1981)

2+9 set departs from Dufftown with a Hertfordshire 'Highland Fling' railtour which had started from Aberdeen and would finish at Kings Cross. Power car 43111 (BG) was leading. (April 1990/Roddy MacPhee)

2+8 set at Edinburgh with the 0915 service to Kings Cross. Note the rail staff uniforms at the time. How things have changed! (August 1981)

2+7 set thrashes through Kirkconnel with the 1025 Edinburgh to Penzance service, power car 43069 (EC) trailing. (July 1992)

2+8 set north of Lockerbie with a diverted Edinburgh to Kings Cross service. The ECML was closed due to engineering work. (February 1985)

2+9 set at Moy north of Aviemore with an Inverness to Kings Cross service, power car 43061 (NL) trailing. (August 2019/Roddy MacPhee)

An interior view of an HST cab at the east end of Edinburgh ready to depart to Kings Cross with the second man enjoying his pipe! (August 1981)

2+8 set departs Montrose heading south with an Aberdeen to Kings Cross service, power car 43158 (BG) trailing. (July 1987)

2+9 set in East Midlands livery at Culloden with an Inverness to Kings Cross service. (April 2012/Roddy MacPhee)

The Network Rail Measurement Train arriving in Edinburgh, power car 43067 (DT) leading. Note the Class 322 stabled in the sidings behind the train. These were used on the North Berwick services at this time. (August 2005)

2+8 set arrives at Perth with an Inverness to Kings Cross service, power car 43090 (EC) leading. Note the first-class coaches immediately behind the loco. (August 1984)

2+8 set near Culloden south of Inverness with an Inverness to Kings Cross service, power car 43107 (NL) trailing. (July 1997/Roddy MacPhee)

HST and a Class 47 at Glasgow Central. The HST was on a CrossCountry service to Poole and the 47 was taking ECS to Polmadie Depot. Any expansion of the station would require several buildings on the right to be demolished – difficult but not impossible. (May 1982)

2+4 set at Gollanfield near Invernes Airport with an Inverness to Aberdeen service, power car 43026 leading. (January 2019/Roddy MacPhee)

2+9 Midland Pullman set at Ayr with a day excursion to Scarborough. Note the tarpaulin around part of the Station Hotel. This part of the hotel was fire damaged by arsonists in 2023 and was removed by a demolition squad by June 2024. (May 2022)

2+8 set arrives at Montrose with a Kings Cross to Aberdeen service with set 254023 (NL). Note the line behind the station on the right. This allowed freight trains to be by-passed but was removed during re-signalling work in 2010. (August 1980)

2+7 set takes the Annbank route north of Mauchline with a diverted Poole to Glasgow Central service. No path was available via Kilmarnock due to single line constraints which is still the same today. Power car 43070 (EC) was trailing. (May 1996)

2+4 set at Tomatin near Aviemore in the snow with an Inverness to Edinburgh service, power car 43152 (HA) leading. (February 2021/Roddy MacPhee)

2+7 set passes over Kilmarnock Viaduct with the Sunday 1025 Edinburgh to Penzance service, power car 43098 (EC) leading. (July 1992)

2+8 set at Wallyford on the ECML with an Aberdeen to Kings Cross service, power car 43084 (NL) leading. (November 1990/Roddy MacPhee)

2+9 set approaches Mussleburgh with a Kings Cross to Aberdeen service. (June 2004)

2+8 set north of Lockerbie with a diverted Edinburgh to Kings Cross service. The ECML was closed due to engineering work. (February 1985)

2+8 set at Montrose North signal box with the 0720 Aberdeen to Kings Cross service. This signal box took over Montrose South and Usan areas of Control in 2010 and was simply re-named Montrose. (August 1981)

2+9 set at Culloden south of Inverness in East Midlands livery with an Inverness to Kings Cross service, power car 43043 (NL) leading. (May 2016/Roddy MacPhee)

2+7 set at New Cumnock with the Sunday 1025 Edinburgh to Penzance. This station re-opened to passengers in May 1991. (September 1992)

2+8 set in GNER livery arrives at Haymarket with a Leeds to Aberdeen service. Note the car park on the left. This was removed in 2006 to make way for an additional platform and also later lines were added for the tram system. (January 2001)

2+4 set at Queen Street with the 0710 Queen Street to Inverness service, power car 43135 (HA) leading. (May 2019)

2+8 set pulls up the steep gradient south of Montrose and crosses the River Esk on the single line to Usan with an Aberdeen to Kings Cross service. This viaduct has fourteen arches. (December 1982)

2+7 set at Bowhouse near Hurlford between Kilmarnock and Dumfries with a diverted Glasgow Central to Poole service, power car 43081(EC) leading. (May 1996)

2+9 Midland Pullman set at Polnish on the West Highland Line with a special from Fort William to Mallaig. (October 2021/Roddy MacPhee)

2+7 set in Virgin livery near Lamington on the WCML with a Glasgow Central to Poole service. (September 2001)

2+8 set near Dunbar with an Edinburgh to Kings Cross service. (July 1981)

2+7 set passes Kirkconnel signal box and station with a diverted Glasgow Central to Paignton service, power car 43082 (EC) leading. (July 1992)

2+8 set departs from Edinburgh with the 1700 service to London Kings Cross. Taken from Calton Hill. This area has changed beyond recognition. There are rumours that Transport Scotland want to re-double the track through the Mound Tunnels and four track the ECML to Drem and possibly beyond. (May 1982/Paul Strathdee)

2+7 set near Cummertrees between Annan and Gretna Junction with the Sunday 1025 Edinburgh to Penzance service, power car 43079 (NL) trailing. This section of line was re-doubled in 2007 mainly to meet the growing demand for coal trains. (April 1993)

2+7 set north of Auchinleck with a diverted Birmingham New Street to Glasgow Central working. The service had been diverted due to a freight train derailment on the WCML near Quintinshill. (August 1998)

Inverness Station. On the left 43168 (HA) has arrived trailing on a service from Queen Street. On the right 43143 (HA) leading awaits departure with a service to Aberdeen. It was substituting for a failed Class 158. (January 2021/Roddy MacPhee)

2+9 set at Johnstone with a special train organised by Hertfodshire Railtours. It was en route from Nottingham to Glasgow Central, power car 43066 (NL) leading. (November 1991)

2+9 Midland Pullman set at Kilmarnock. It had been stabled overnight from a previous working from Llandudno to Ayr. It later ran ECS back to its base at Crewe. (June 2021)

2+8 set at Carrbridge with a Kings Cross to Inverness service, power car 43105 (BG) leading. Note all coaches except the rear power car were in GNER livery. (April 1997/Roddy MacPhee)

2+5 set with 43026 (HA) leading sprints through Springfield with the 0930 Edinburgh to Aberdeen service. Rear power car was 43032 (HA). This station only has two stopping trains in either direction Monday to Saturday with nothing on a Sunday, These are known as 'Parliamentary Trains'. No attempt appears to be getting made by Transport Scotland to stop more of the local services between Edinburgh and Dundee. (September 2024)

2+7 set near Lugton with a diverted Glasgow Central to Birmingham New Street service, power car 43052 (EC) leading. Note the Ex Caledonian line bridge abutment from Neilston to Kilwinning and Ardrossan Montgomery Pier at the rear coach. This line closed to passengers in 1949 and the track was lifted by the mid-1950s. (March 1992)

2+7 set crosses Culloden Viaduct south of Inverness with an Inverness to Kings Cross service. This was a CrossCountry set on hire to East Coast after the booked LNER set had failed the previous day on the *Highland Chieftan*. (May 2014/Roddy MacPhee)

2+4 set with 43034 (HA) leading at Leuchars with the 0831 Edinburgh to Aberdeen service. Rear power car was 43033 (HA). (June 2024)

2+9 set at Garrochburn north of Mauchline with a railtour named the 'Thames-Clyde Express' en route from London St Pancras to Glasgow Central, power car 43163 (BG) leading. The farm in the distance is Mossgiel and was once the home to the poet Robert Burns. (March 1992)

2+8 set arrives in Edinburgh with a service from Leeds. (May 1986)

The Network Rail Measurement Train stabled between duties at Falkland Yard Ayr. Note the coal wagons still in use at the time. Sadly now just a memory. (August 2009)

2+5 set at Boat of Garten. This was a special ScotRail Santa service that had operated from Edinburgh and was about to return back home. (December 2021/Roddy MacPhee)

2+5 set, power car 43093 (NL) trailing arrives at Central with a service from Manchester Piccadilly. (November 2002)

2+4 set at Crubenmore near Kingussie with an Inverness to Perth ScotRail driver training run. (May 2018/Roddy MacPhee)

2+8 set at Aberdeen having just arrived with the 1000 from Kings Cross. Note the GUV parcel coach to the right. (August 1984)

2+4 set passes through Laurencekirk with an Edinburgh to Aberdeen service, power car 43015 (HA) leading. This station closed in September 1967 and re-opened in May 2009. (September 2023)

2+8 set passes Beattock Summit with a diverted Edinburgh to Kings Cross service. This was due to the ECML being closed for engineering work. (February 1985)

2+4 set at Kinveachy between Carrbridge and Aviemore on the first day of ScotRail driver training with a special working running from Inverness to Perth, power car 43132 (HA) leading. (May 2018/Roddy MacPhee)

2+9 set at Ayr station with a special organised by Hertfodshire Railtours. It was en route from London St Pancras to Stranraer Harbour, power car 43043 (NL) leading. (March 1993)

2+5 set arrives Haymarket with the 0730 Edinburgh to Aberdeen service, power car 43145 (HA) leading. This station has changed beyond all recognition since the 1980s. (June 2024)

2+7 set near Abington with a CrossCountry service from Glasgow Central to Poole, power car 43090 (EC) leading. (July 1991)

2+7 set in Virgin livery at Barony north of Auchinleck with a diverted Glasgow Central to Poole service, power car 43099 (EC) leading. (August 1998)

2+9 Midland Pullman set at Kinloid near Arisaig with a special from Mallaig to Fort William, power car 43055 (LS) leading. (October 2021/Roddy MacPhee)

2+8 set approaches Paisley Gilmour Street with an advertised day excursion from Nottingham, power car 43104 (NL) *County of Cleveland* leading. It was later renumbered 43304 and worked with East Midland Trains. (April 1989)

2+5 set at Dalmeny with an Edinburgh to Aberdeen service, power car 43141 (HA) leading. (May 2019)

2+8 set at Cradlehall with an Inverness to Kings Cross service, power car 43054 (NL) leading. It was passing 37421 (IS) which was on an engineers' train. (November 1989/Roddy MacPhee)

2+8 set emerges out of the Calton Tunnel Edinburgh with a Leeds to Aberdeen service, power car 43277 (NL) leading. (February 2009/Paul Strathdee)

2+8 set at Inverness with the *Highland Chieftan*. This departed on a Sunday at 1005 for Kings Cross. (April 1987/Roddy MacPhee)

2+4 set approaches Kinghorn with an Edinburgh to Aberdeen service, power car 43136 (HA) leading. (August 2023)

2+9 set near Dalwhinnie with an Inverness to Kings Cross service, power car 43318 (NL) leading. (May 2018/Roddy MacPhee)

2+7 set passes Kirkconnel signal box and station with the Sunday 1025 Edinburgh to Penzance service, power car 43082 (EC) leading. (July 1992)

2+4 set arrives at North Queensferry with an Aberdeen to Edinburgh service, power car 43183 (HA) leading. (August 2023)

2+7 set hurtles through Carluke station with a CrossCountry service from Newcastle to Glasgow Central, power car 43041 (NL) leading. (July 1991)

2+8 set at Aberdeen with a service to Kings Cross, power car 43079 (EC) trailing. Note the BG parcel coach to the left. (August 1984)

2+5 set passes through South Gyle with an Aberdeen to Edinburgh service, power car 43133 (HA) leading. In the background you can just about see Edinburgh Gateway station which is the official connecting station for the airport. (August 2023)

2+5 set at Avielochan near Aviemore with an Edinburgh to Inverness service. (April 2023/Roddy MacPhee)

2+8 set at Burnmouth with the 1515 Edinburgh to Kings Cross service. (July 1981)

2+4 set at Croy with the 0536 Inverness to Queen Street service, power car 43130 (HA) leading. Note the new overbridge with lifts. This has become the new standard practice at most stations but many of them always seem to be out of order! (July 2024)

2+8 set at Beattock with a diverted Leeds to Edinburgh service. Attempts to re-open this station have fallen on deaf ears over the years despite the population being larger than Reston or East Linton. (February 1985)

2+8 set at Aviemore with a special en route from Inverness to Edinburgh, power car 43206 (NL) leading. This set had been specially re-painted for the LNER Farewell railtour. (December 2019/ Roddy MacPhee)

2+4 set approaches Dundee with a Queen Street to Aberdeen service, power car 43127 (HA) leading. (September 2023)

2+8 set at Edinburgh in Virgin livery, power car 43065 (EC) *City of Edinburgh* trailing. It was working an Edinburgh to Bournemouth service. (April 2002)

2+4 set passes through Broughty Ferry with an Aberdeen to Edinburgh Service, power car 43136 (HA) leading. The old signal box has been superbly restored. (September 2023)

2+9 Midland Pullman set stabled in the Long Lye sidings at Kilmarnock. These tracks originally went onto Dalry via Crosshouse but were closed in May 1976. The remaining sidings were used by coal trains until 2019 but now only see the odd special and Sprinter ECS moves. The line to Barrhead can just about be seen behind the jungle of trees. (May 2022)

2+4 set arrives at Montrose with an Aberdeen to Queen Street service, power car 43021 (HA) leading. (September 2023)

2+5 set arrives in Perth Platform No 2 with a Queen Street to Aberdeen service, power car 43183 (HA) leading. The line becomes single and crosses the River Tay just behind the camera for approximately 1 mile to Barnhill Junction. (July 2023)

2+9 Midland Pullman set approaches Barassie Junction with ECS from Crewe to Falkland Yard Ayr. The ECS then stabled overnight and worked a day excursion from Newton On Ayr to Scarborough the next day. (November 2023)

2+4 set at Crubenmore near Dalwhinnie with an Inverness to Queen Street service, power car 43030 (HA) leading. (June 2019/Roddy MacPhee)

2+5 set in Virgin livery approaches Glasgow Central with a service from Bournemouth. These short formed sets worked during the Voyager introduction before being withdrawn. (November 2002)

2+5 set arrives at Montrose with an Aberdeen to Queen Street service, power car 43133 (HA) leading. This power car was badly damaged during severe gales near Broughty Ferry in January 2024 when a large tree was blown onto it. The train had been travelling at approximately 85 mph. Fortunately, the driver survived showing once again the ruggedness of the original design. (September 2023)

2+4 set at Edinburgh Park with the 0638 Inverness to Edinburgh service, power car 43015 (HA) leading with 43146 (HA) trailing. This station opened up to rail traffic in December 2003 and also now has a convenient tram link nearby. (September 2024)

2+8 set in GNER livery at Haymarket with the 0700 Leeds to Aberdeen service power car 43208 (NH) leading. (June 2008)

2+5 set passes through Portlethan with a Queen Street to Aberdeen service, power car 43134 (HA) leading. This station was re-opened in May 2009. (September 2023)

2+7 set at arrives at Central with a service from Paignton, power car 43100 (EC) leading. (April 1999)

2+4 set at Delnies near Nairn with an Inverness to Aberdeen service, power car 43129 (HA) leading. (July 2020/Roddy MacPhee)

2+4 set departs Perth with an Inverness to Edinburgh service, power car 43177 (HA) leading. (July 2023)

2+7 set at Barrhead signal box with the Sunday 1025 Edinburgh to Penzance service, power car 43081 (EC) leading. This box was closed in November 2023 and all work transferred to the WSCC at Springburn Glasgow. (June 1992)

2+8 set passes Pettycur Bay near Burntisland with an Aberdeen to Kings Cross service. (June 1984/Matt Scott)

2+4 set at Gleneagles with the 0639 Aberdeen to Queen Street service, power car 43021 (HA) leading. (July 2024)

The Network Rail Measurement Train passes the site of the new Inverness Airport with an Inverness to Dundee working, power car 43251 (DT) trailing. (August 2022/Roddy MacPhee)

2+4 set passes through Aberdour with an Edinburgh to Aberdeen service, power car 43003 (HA) leading. (August 2023)

An interior view of one of the refurbished HST MK3 ScotRail first-class coaches. (September 2023)

2+8 set at Wallyford in LNER livery hurries through with an Aberdeen to Kings Cross service, power car 43320 (NL) leading. Wallyford station re-opened in June 1994. (September 2018)

2+4 set passes through Dalgety Bay with an Aberdeen to Edinburgh service, power car 43124 (HA) leading. This station was re-opened in March 1998. (August 2023)

2+8 set at Abington with a diverted Edinburgh to Kings Cross service. The ECML was closed due to engineering work. (February 1985)

2+4 set at Dalnaspidal between Blair Atholl and Dalwhinnie with an Edinburgh to Inverness service, power car 43125 (HA) leading. (August 2020/Roddy MacPhee)

2+9 Midland Pullman set at Craigens near Cumnock between Kilmarnock and Dumfries with a day excursion from Ayr to Scarborough, power car 43046 (LS) leading *Geoff Drury 1930–1999*. (May 2022)

2+4 set with power car 43142 (HA) leading at Ladybank with the 0930 Edinburgh to Aberdeen service. Power car 43151 was on the rear. (June 2024)

2+9 set arrives at Falkirk Grahamston, power car 43239 (NL) leading. It was working the 'Highland Chieftan' service from Inverness to Kings Cross. (February 2019)

Power cars 43143 and 43012 (both HA) rest between duties at their home depot. From the end of 2024, more trains were formed up to 2+5 from 2+4 sets. (September 2024)

2+8 set passes the site of the former Penmanshiel Tunnel with a Kings Cross to Edinburgh service. Note the remains of the original A1 road. The tunnel collapsed in March 1979, entombing two engineers, resulting in both the track and road having to be re-aligned. (July 1981)

2+5 set passes through Invergowrie with an Aberdeen to Queen Street service. Power car 43125 (HA) leading. (July 2023)

2+9 set at Tomatin near Aviemore with an Inverness to Kings Cross service, power car 43305 (NL) leading. (January 2018/Roddy MacPhee)

2+8 set at Aberdeen with the 1200 service to Kings Cross. Note the freightliner terminal on the right, now long gone. (August 1981)

2+4 set passes Carnoustie with an Aberdeen to Edinburgh service, power car 43147 (HA) leading. (September 2023)

2+8 set in LNER livery arrives at Dalmeny with an Aberdeen to Kings Cross service, power car 43316 (NL) leading. (May 2019)

2+4 set passes Laurencekirk signal box with an Aberdeen to Edinburgh service, power car 43177 (HA) leading. (September 2023)

2+7 Midland Pullman set at Moy near Aviemore with a special from Inverness to Slough. (March 2022/Roddy MacPhee)

The Network Rail Measurement Train at Glasgow Central with 43013 (DT) *Mark Carne OBE* leading. It was working around the Glasgow area. On this occasion its next move was to Edinburgh via Shotts. (May 2019)

2+8 set passes Polmadie Depot on the south side of Glasgow with a diverted Glasgow Central to Kings Cross working. This was due to engineering work around Queen Street. Power cars on this occasion were 43067 leading and 43073 trailing (both EC). (April 1982)

2+4 set departs Stirling with an Aberdeen to Queen Street service, power car 43152 (HA) trailing. (September 2023)

2+8 set approaches Perth with the 1200 London Kings Cross to Inverness service, power car 43198 (NL) leading. (April 1986/Paul Strathdee)

2+8 set at Haymarket with a Kings Cross to Aberdeen service, power car 43308 (NL) leading. This power car was named *Highland Chieftan*. It was formerly numbered 43108. (May 2019)

47677 (IS) departs from Inverness station with a Kings Cross working. The 47 was assisting this set due to one of the HST power cars having failed and would take the train as far south as Perth. (August 1992/Roddy MacPhee)

2+4 set passes Carnoustie signal box. It was working an Aberdeen to Edinburgh service, power car 43030 (HA) trailing. (September 2023)

2+4 set approaches the Forth Bridge with an Edinburgh to Aberdeen service whilst a Fife Circle service worked by a Class 170 heads south to Edinburgh. (May 2019)

2+9 Midland Pullman set at Kilmarnock, power car 43055 (LS) trailing with an excursion from Newton On Ayr to Scarborough. The train was supposed to start from Ayr but could not do so reaction to the adjacent station hotel being unsafe due to fire damage. (November 2023)

2+8 set at Musselburgh with an Aberdeen to Leeds service. This station was re-opened in October 1988. (June 2004)

2+8 set near Burnmouth with the 1000 Kings Cross to Edinburgh service 'The Flying Scotsman'. (July 1981)

2+5 set at Larbert with the 0838 Edinburgh to Inverness service, power car 43179 (HA) leading. (July 2024)

2+4 set at Tomatin near Aviemore with a Queen Street to Inverness service, power car 43131 (HA) leading. (August 2022/Roddy MacPhee)

2+4 set approaches Invergowrie with a Queen Street to Aberdeen service, power car 43151 (HA) leading. (July 2023)

2+8 set with power car 43122 (NL) *South Yorkshire Metropolitan County* leading at Greenock Central with a return excursion from Gourock to Nottingham. (April 1989)

The Network Rail Measurement Train near Mauchline heading south with a Mossend Yard to Derby RTC working. It had been diverted from the WCML due to bridge damage at Lamington. (February 2016)

2+4 set at Queen Street, power car 43149 (HA) trailing with a morning service to Inverness. (May 2019)

2+4 set at Dalnaspidal between Blair Atholl and Dalwhinnie with an Edinburgh to Inverness service, power car 43149 (NL) trailing. (October 2019/Roddy MacPhee)

2+8 set at Wallyford in LNER livery streaking through with a Kings Cross to Edinburgh service. Wallyford station re-opened in June 1994. (September 2018)

2+5 set passes through Portlethan with a Queen Street to Aberdeen service, power car 43134 (HA) leading. This station was re-opened in May 2009. (September 2023)

2+9 Midland Pullman set near Gatehead between Kilmarnock and Barassie with a return excursion from Llandudno to Ayr, power car 43055 (LS) leading. (June 2021)

2+4 set approaches Dundee with an Edinburgh to Aberdeen service, power car 43142 (HA) leading. It is about to coast down the steep gradient towards the station. (July 2023)

2+4 set at Gollanfield near Nairn with an Inverness to Aberdeen service, power car 43012 (HA) trailing. (September 2019/Roddy MacPhee)

2+7 set at Lugton signal box with the Sunday 1025 Edinburgh to Penzance service, power car 43067 (EC) with buffers leading. (June 1992)

2+8 set crosses Slochd Viaduct north of Aviemore with an Inverness to Kings Cross service. Note the maintenance workers hanging over the side of the structure. (June 2018/Roddy MacPhee)

2+4 set arrives at Stirling with an Aberdeen to Queen Street service, power car 43150 (HA) leading. (September 2023)

2+8 set arrives at Haymarket in GNER livery with an Aberdeen to Kings Cross service. Note the new Platform 0 to the right. (April 2006)

2+4 set passes through Kinghorn with an Edinburgh to Aberdeen service, power car 43124 (HA) trailing. (August 2023)

2+8 set at Larbert Junction with the midday London Kings Cross to Inverness service. (May 1988/Paul Strathdee)

2+4 set approaches Aviemore with a Driver's Trainer from Perth to Inverness, power car 43140 (HA) leading. This was the last day of semaphore signals at Aviemore. (March 2019/Roddy MacPhee)

37667 (DR) in the snow just south of Inverness drags a failed HST. The service was booked to Kings Cross but the loco would only take the failure as far as Edinburgh where a replacement HST took over. (January 2010/Roddy MacPhee)

2+4 set at Dundee with an Aberdeen to Edinburgh service, power car 43152 (HA) leading. The adjacent by-pass line nearer to the retaining wall was removed in the early 1990s. (September 2023)

2+4 set on the Network Rail Measurement Train, power car 43274 (DT) trailing arrives at Kilmarnock with an Ayr to Derby RTC working. This and the front power car were bought from LNER. (March 2023)

2+4 set departs North Queensferry with an Aberdeen to Edinburgh service, power car 43152 (HA) trailing. (August 2023)

Power car 43127 (HA) seen outside Inverness station in the process of being turned via a ground frame and triangle. This was probably when it was getting re-formed into a new set. (January 2021/Roddy MacPhee)

2+9 Midland Pullman set north of Auchinleck with a set of ECS from Falkland Yard to Crewe Sidings. Hard to believe that there was a mine with four sidings to the left of the leading power car. This was Barony Colliery which closed in 1983. (November 2023)

2+7 set near Powfoot in heavy rain north of Annan with the diverted 1255 Birmingham New Street to Edinburgh service. Note the leading power car 43079 (NL) had been modified with buffers for use as a surrogate DVT on the ECML with Class 91 locos. (April 1993)

2+4 set approaches Carnoustie signal box and station with an Edinburgh to Aberdeen service, power car 43026 (HA) leading. (September 2023)

2+8 set at Inverness station stabled in the adjacent sidings, power car 43112 (NL) leading. It was booked to work the LNER HST farewell tour the next day. (December 2019/Roddy MacPhee)